EZRA'S QUEST

FOLLOW THAT DOG!

FOLLOW
THAT DOG!

Join Ezra now in days of yore,
Thirteen hundred ninety-four.
Through the window swirls a fog.
An arm grabs Ezra's faithful dog!
Who took the pup? Find out! Win praise!
Spot clues in this medieval maze!

A Doubleday Book for Young Readers

EZRA'S QUEST

ROSALYN SCHANZER

A Doubleday Book for Young Readers
Published by
Delacorte Press
Bantam Doubleday Dell Publishing Group, Inc.
1540 Broadway
New York, New York 10036
Doubleday and the portrayal of an anchor with a dolphin are
trademarks of Bantam Doubleday Dell Publishing Group, Inc.
Copyright © 1994 by Rosalyn Schanzer

Library of Congress Cataloging in Publication Data
Schanzer, Rosalyn.
Ezra's quest : Follow that dog! / Rosalyn Schanzer.
p.   cm.
"A Doubleday book for young readers."
Summary: In order to find his dog, a boy must make his way
through a series of mazes each of which is accompanied by
information about life in medieval times.
ISBN 0-385-32262-3
1. Maze puzzles—Juvenile literature.   [1. Maze puzzles.
2. Puzzles.   3. Middle Ages.]   I. Title.
GV1507.M3S34   1994
793.73—dc20   93-19537   CIP   AC

Typography by Lynn Braswell

Manufactured in the United States of America

October 1994
10   9   8   7   6   5   4   3   2   1

To the illustrators
of the fabulous
fourteenth-century illuminated manuscripts,
whose work inspired
many of the pictures in this book

Soldiers armed with spear and sword
Attack the castle of a lord.
Ezra saves the noble's daughter—
Evil knights had almost caught her!

START

ZOUNDS! WHO HATH TAKEN MY SHIELD?

MINE, TOO, IS GONE! 'TWAS HERE ONE MOMENT PAST!

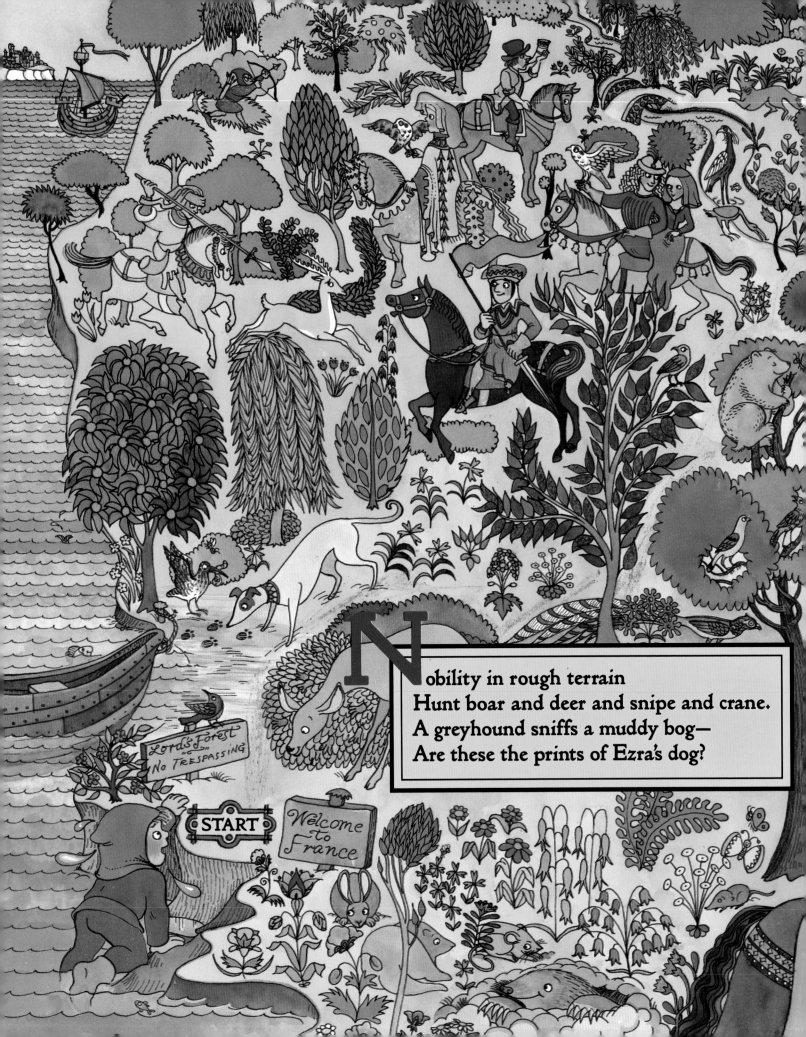

Nobility in rough terrain
Hunt boar and deer and snipe and crane.
A greyhound sniffs a muddy bog—
Are these the prints of Ezra's dog?

Lord's Forest
No TRESPASSING

START

Welcome
to
France

Just outside a city wall,
A candlemaker can recall
That someone holding apples raced
Through crooked streets—oh, pray, give chase!

Could that be Ezra's dog who calls
From deep inside the palace walls?
Quick! Cross the moat! Approach the gate!
Look—giant footprints! Don't be late!

START

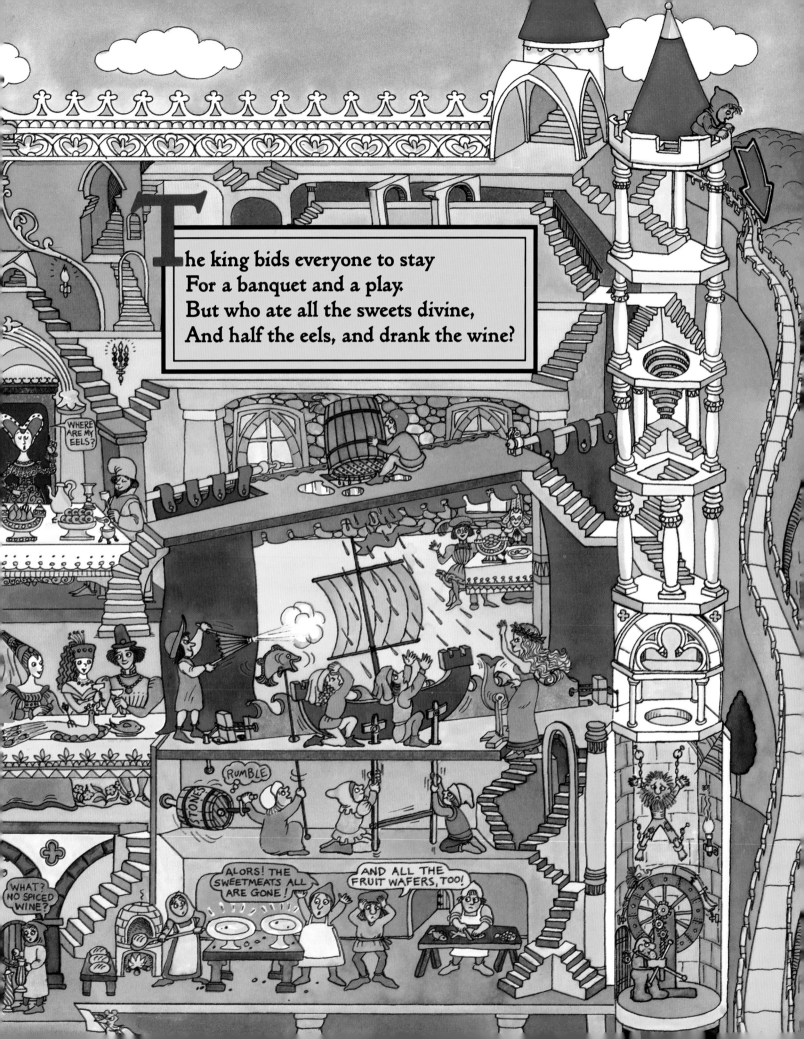

The king bids everyone to stay
For a banquet and a play.
But who ate all the sweets divine,
And half the eels, and drank the wine?

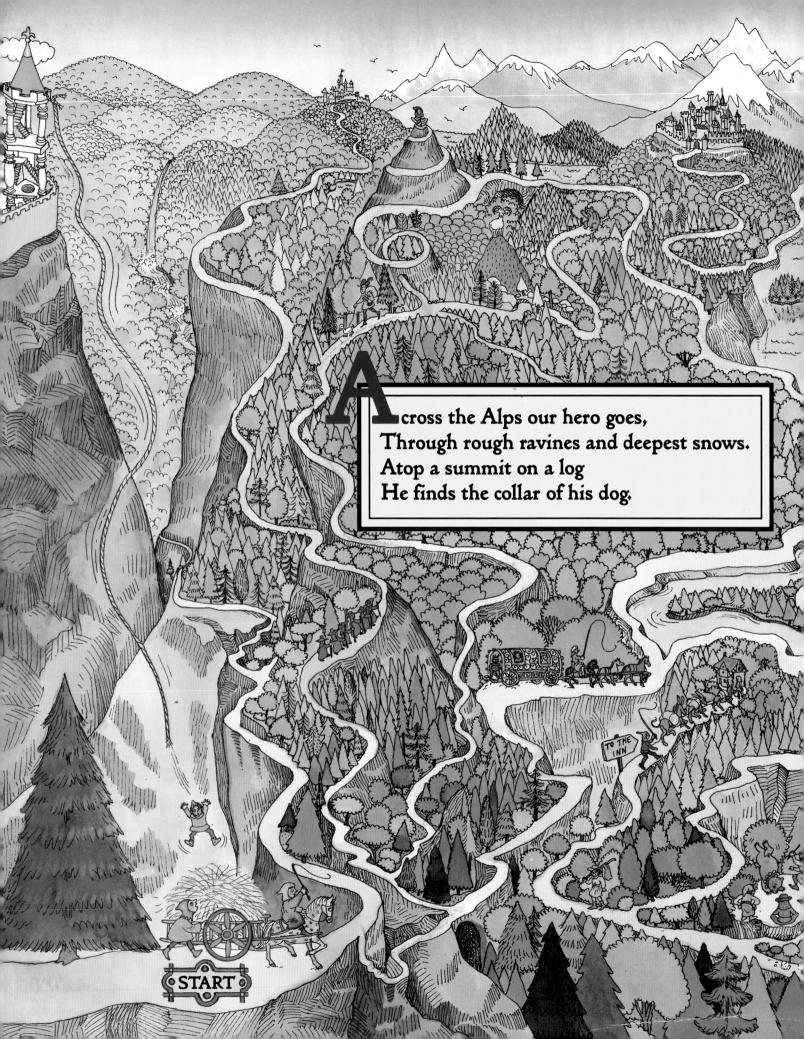

Across the Alps our hero goes,
Through rough ravines and deepest snows.
Atop a summit on a log
He finds the collar of his dog.

TO THE INN

START

Avoid the village, hold your breath;
Bubonic plague could cause Black Death.
"Behold," two woodsmen cry. "Forsooth!
Could this be some enormous tooth?"

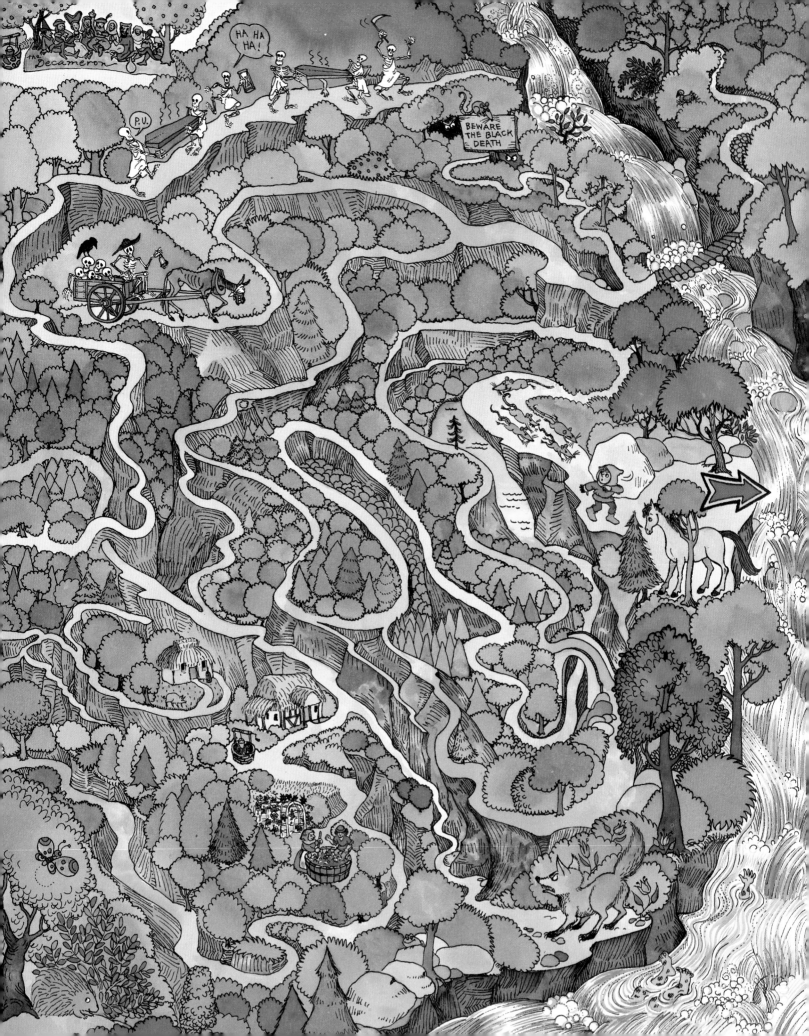

On yonder cliff there looms a tower.
Ezra runs with all his power.
Atop stone stairs, behind a door
He hearkens to a fearsome roar!

START

Inside the room's a big surprise;
A dragon sleeps with smiling eyes.
His roar's a snore, and in his arm,
The dog sleeps smiling, safe and warm.

Ezra wakes the sleepers up.
"What happened?" he says to his pup.
"We had fun!" the dog replies.
"He's my friend!" the dragon cries.

Through the pageant of medieval history rode minstrels and magicians, knights and knaves, monks and milkmaids, and witches and wizards. Robin Hood, the legendary English outlaw who robbed from the rich and gave to the poor, was first mentioned in writing in 1378. Rollicking tales by Geoffrey Chaucer and Giovanni Boccaccio parodied daily life, and bizarre demons and devils materialized in an epic poem, *The Divine Comedy* by Dante Alighieri.

The Hundred Years' War between England and France was fought by knights wearing fifty-five-pound armor and dark, stuffy helmets weighing eleven pounds. Each wielded a lance, two swords, a dagger, a battle-ax with spike, and a mace. Many also had longbows or guns. Castles were the primary targets. Armies scaled walls and fired missiles from below. Castles were defended from towers behind formidable double curtain walls.

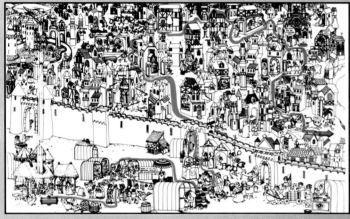

Walled cities teemed with craftsmen, beggars, merchants wearing Oriental silks, pickpockets, alchemists, students, sailors, fat oxen, pet monkeys, squawking chickens, and royal processions. There were fairs, public markets, enormous street signs advertising services, noisy taverns, fountains fed by aqueducts, and lofty cathedrals. Garbage was tossed from the windows of narrow half-timbered houses, and hired workers raked manure from city streets.

A king's palace grounds encompassed orchards, fish ponds graced by swans, herb and flower gardens, and vine-covered courtyards containing exotic beasts from across the seas. Chivalry and courtly love ruled the day. Noblemen and ladies flirted in fragrant groves of orange trees, while princesses perched on balconies were serenaded by dashing knights. Youths and maidens in rich array sang, danced, and played harmonies on lutes, flutes, harps, bagpipes, or zithers.

Roads were filled with travelers. Merchants in pack trains, noble ladies or sick people in carriages, armies on horseback, couriers carrying letters for a fee, pilgrims, peddlers, bishops, tax collectors, flagellants, robber barons, and highwaymen all rode or walked on roads that rarely had signposts or bridges. They could be rutted, muddy, dusty, or paved with stones. Mountaineers and monks strung ropes along mountain ridges to ease travel through the snowy Alps.

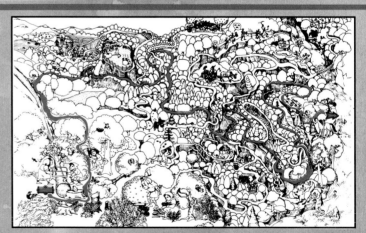

Rats and fleas were the carriers of the infamous Black Death that swept through Europe during the 1300s, killing up to half the population. Victims had big black lumps or splotches and died within one to five days. Parisian nuns were among the tiny number who dared to risk their lives by treating the sick. Some villagers danced to trumpets and drums in a vain effort to avoid the plague "by the jollity that is in us."

During the Middle Ages, most land was owned by powerful lords. Peasants grew their lord's food as well as their own, tended his property, and paid him many kinds of rents and taxes. In return, the lord provided land use, protection from invaders, and criminal and legal justice. His poorest serfs ate bread and onions and slept on straw; wealthier peasants had many acres of land, feather beds, and dowries for their daughters.

Large parties of nobility hunted in the lords' forests wearing cloaks trimmed with ermine and pearls or squirrel-skin coats adorned with bells. Horses were richly bedecked, and even the greyhounds wore velvet collars. Falcons trained to aid in the hunt sported silver bells. So much land was deforested for grazing and farming that these private forests became a last refuge for many wild animals.

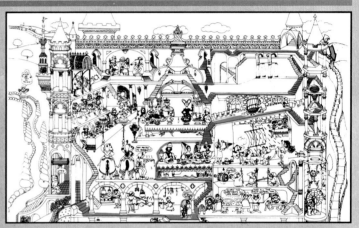

Jousting tournaments made spectacular public entertainment. Heralds trumpeted the arrival of scores of knights bearing banners and garbed in crested helmets and armor glittering with jewels. Richly draped horses wore armor as well. The object of the joust was often more to gain favor from the ladies than it was to knock one's opponent off his horse, but losers had to give their horses and armor to the winners.

Royal banquets embraced hundreds of guests glutting themselves on such extravagant delicacies as swans with gilded beaks resting on spun-sugar landscapes, venison and fish aspics, spiced wine served by nobles on horseback, fruit wafers, civet of hare, and sweetmeats showered from the ceiling in scented artificial rain. Plays were enlivened by amazing special effects utilizing trapdoors, weights, pulleys, cascades of water, and real blood and guts from the butcher.

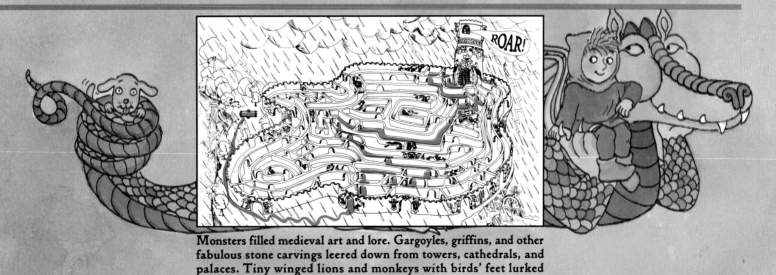

Monsters filled medieval art and lore. Gargoyles, griffins, and other fabulous stone carvings leered down from towers, cathedrals, and palaces. Tiny winged lions and monkeys with birds' feet lurked between the lines of calligraphy in illuminated manuscripts. Some people thought that faraway lands were home to men with dogs' heads, horned pygmies, and monsters with one eye and one foot.

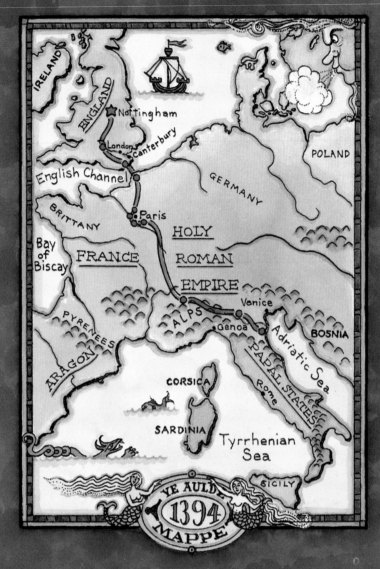

The journey readers take in this book explores many aspects of life in the late Middle Ages, from chivalry and courtly love to feudalism, the Black Death, and the Hundred Years' War. The clothing, armor, weaponry, landscape, and architecture depicted here were researched using both museum artifacts and literature about the period. Many illuminated manuscripts, such as the Lutrell Psalter, were particularly valuable, ensuring the accuracy of each element and evoking a feeling for everyday life. Characters from medieval literature are also hidden in the panoramas on these pages, including Chanticleer and the Fox from Chaucer's *Canterbury Tales*, the demons and devils of Dante's *Divine Comedy*, a picnic scene from Boccaccio's *Decameron*, and Geoffrey Chaucer himself.

ROSALYN SCHANZER is the author/illustrator of *Ezra in Pursuit: The Great Maze Chase*. Her work has appeared in hundreds of books, magazine articles, and posters for children.